Rivers of Europe:

5. Volga
6. Danube
7. Rhine
8. Rhone
9. Po
10. Dneiper

Rivers of ia:

11. Irtys
12. Br
13.
14

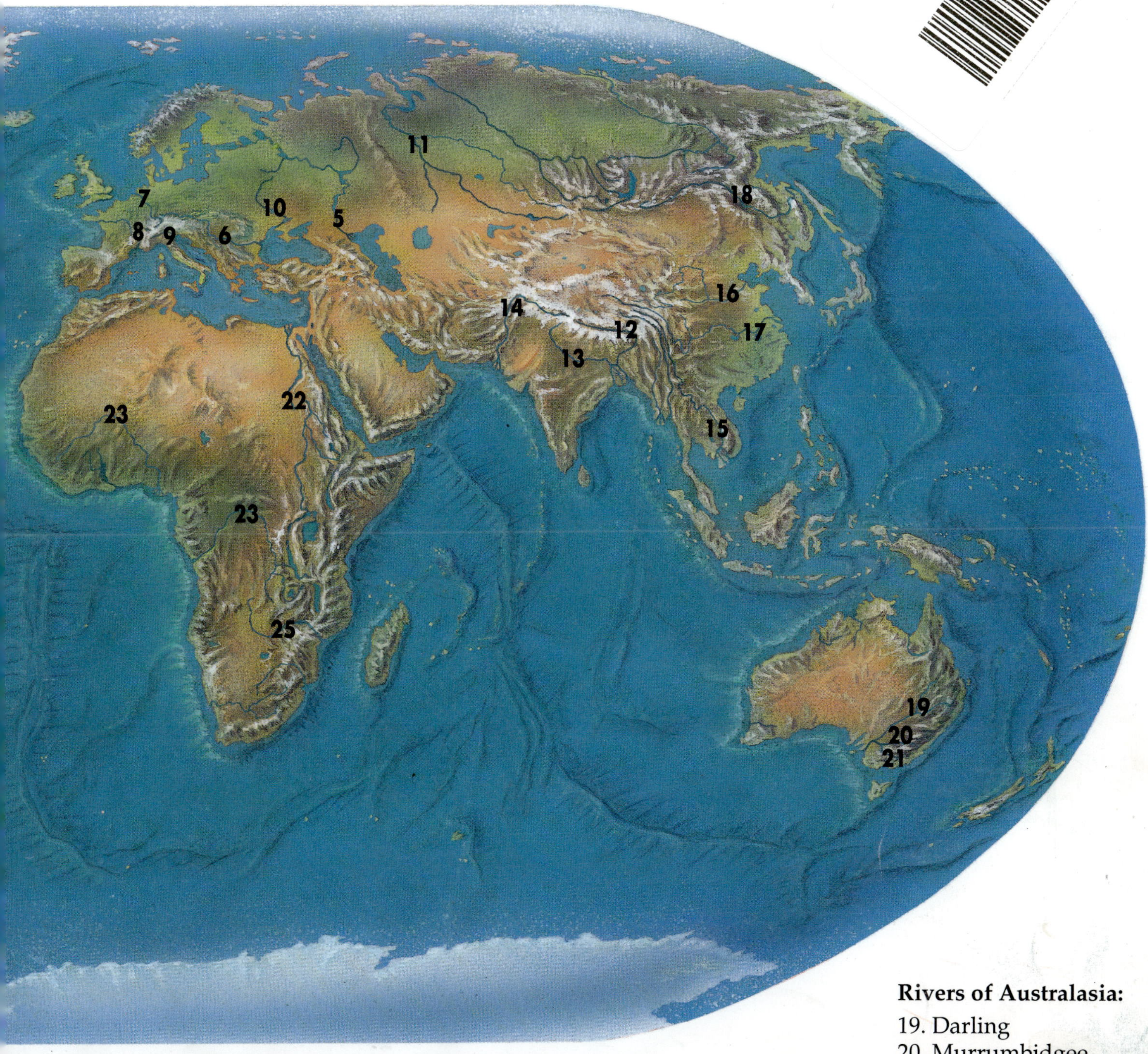

Rivers of Australasia:

19. Darling
20. Murrumbidgee
21. Murray

Rivers of Africa:

22. Nile
23. Zaire
24. Niger
25. Zambesi

Facts about rivers

The world's longest river is the Nile in East Africa, stretching 6670 kilometres from the Equator to the Mediterranean sea. Only slightly shorter are the Amazon (6450 km) in South America, the Yangtze (5950 km) and the Hwang He (4850 km), both in China. The longest river in North America is the Mississippi (3800 km) but it is only the tenth longest river in the world. Europe's longest river is the Volga which runs south through Russia to the Caspian Sea for 3690 kilometres. The longest river in Australia is the Murray (2589 km).

The largest river basin belongs to the River Amazon, stretching over about 7 billion square kilometres, with 15,000 major tributary rivers. Its largest tributary, the Rio Madeira, is the world's fourteenth longest river.

The River Ganges makes the biggest delta (75,000 square kilometres) as it enters the Bay of Bengal in Bangladesh and north east India.

The world's muddiest river is the Hwang He in China. It carries so much silt that the river is always a yellow brown colour. For this reason it is also called the Yellow River. The Hwang He has dropped so much silt on its bed that it now flows many metres above the surrounding land, often flooding and causing great loss of life. For this reason the river is also known as 'China's sorrow'. The Mississippi and the Colorado in the US are also very muddy rivers. The Mississippi delta juts out into the Gulf of Mexico downstream of the city of New Orleans.

ATLANTIC EUROPE
PUBLISHING

LAND SHAPES

RIVER

Author
Brian Knapp, BSc, PhD
Art Director
Duncan McCrae, BSc
Editor
Rita Owen
Special models
Tim Fulford, MA, Head of Design and Technology, Leighton Park School
Illustrator
David Hardy
Print consultants
Landmark Production Consultants Ltd
Printed and bound in Hong Kong
Produced by
EARTHSCAPE EDITIONS

First published in the United Kingdom in 1992
by Atlantic Europe Publishing Company Ltd,
86 Peppard Road, Sonning Common, Reading,
Berkshire, RG4 9RP, UK

British Library Cataloguing in Publication Data

Knapp, Brian
River. – (Landshapes)
1. Rivers – Juvenile literature
I. Title II. Series
551.483

ISBN 1–869860–02–0

Acknowledgements. The publishers would like to thank the following: Leighton Park School, Martin Morris and Redlands County Primary School.

Picture credits. All photographs from the Earthscape Editions photographic library except the following (t=top, b=bottom, l=left, r=right): David Higgs 8/9; United States Geological Survey 29t; ZEFA 17b, 28, 32, 33bl, 33r, 34/35.
Cover picture: North Saskatchewan River, Banff National Park, Alberta, Canada.

In this book you will find some words that have been shown in **bold** type. There is a full explanation of each of these words on page 36.

On many pages you will find experiments that you might like to try for yourself. They have been put in a blue box like this.

In this book km means kilometres and m means metres.

These people appear on a number of pages to help you to know the size of some landshapes.

CONTENTS

Take care near rivers

It is easy to visit streams and rivers to see the landshapes described in this book for yourself. But never go near streams or rivers without an adult. Streams and rivers can be dangerous places for the unwary and deaths have occurred because people have fallen into the water and have been carried away by fast currents.

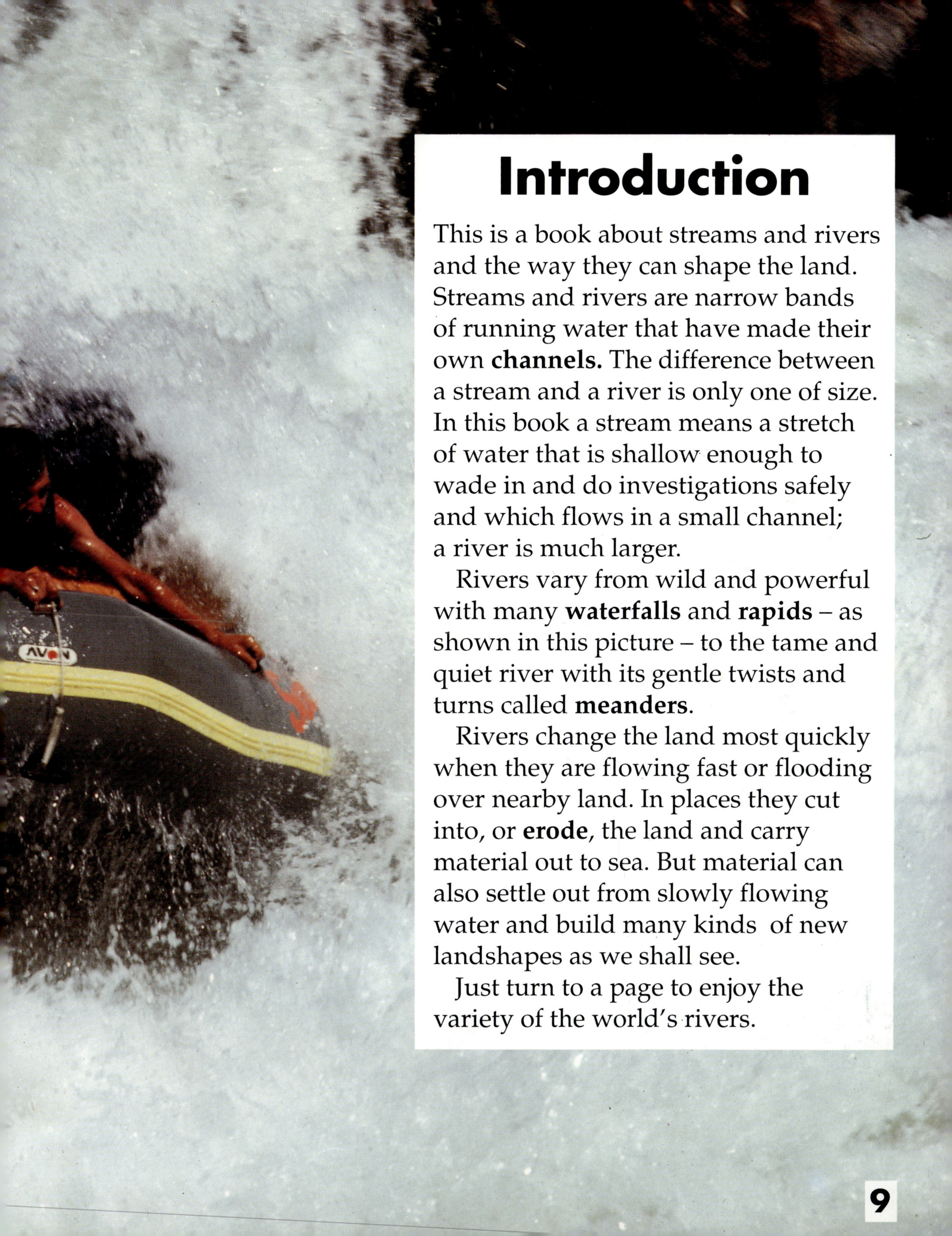

Introduction

This is a book about streams and rivers and the way they can shape the land. Streams and rivers are narrow bands of running water that have made their own **channels.** The difference between a stream and a river is only one of size. In this book a stream means a stretch of water that is shallow enough to wade in and do investigations safely and which flows in a small channel; a river is much larger.

Rivers vary from wild and powerful with many **waterfalls** and **rapids** – as shown in this picture – to the tame and quiet river with its gentle twists and turns called **meanders**.

Rivers change the land most quickly when they are flowing fast or flooding over nearby land. In places they cut into, or **erode**, the land and carry material out to sea. But material can also settle out from slowly flowing water and build many kinds of new landshapes as we shall see.

Just turn to a page to enjoy the variety of the world's rivers.

Chapter 1
How rivers work

Landshapes made by rivers

All rivers flow in a shallow trench or channel that they have cut. Some rivers flow in rocky channels, others flow within channels of muds and silts, sands and gravel or stones and boulders.

Rivers never follow a straight path, but always twist and turn in various patterns, cutting into their banks in some places and filling in their channels elsewhere. This is the way they are able to build the variety of landshapes we shall see on later pages.

Islands are quite common features of a river (see page 22).

Rivers of many patterns
This is a picture of a lowland river. The river has swept over the bottom of the valley many times, leaving signs of its former channels.

When this picture was taken the river was at low water. During floods it will spill over all the flat land in the valley bottom.

The outside of a bend is usually being scoured away (see page 26).

Rivers often change course, leaving signs of their former channels as marshland or **oxbow** lakes (see page 26).

The river often makes a wide flat area in the bottom of a valley. It is called a flood plain (see page 28).

Rivers drop material on the inside of a bend (see page 24).

You cannot see into this water because it is carrying so much fine material eroded from upstream (see page 14).

Follow the flow

It is not easy to see the patterns of water flow in a channel.

Here are some simple ways in which you and your friends can investigate the flow in a small stream or even a large river.

Be environment friendly

Dog biscuits will slowly dissolve in the water without harming the environment and you do not have to worry about collecting them again. You could use natural pine cones or sticks, but do not use plastic or other materials that might remain to pollute the stream.

Floating by

You can easily see how surface water moves by using some simple floats, such as hard dog biscuits, each with a different colour.

Stand in the stream (or stand on a bridge if the stream is deep) with some friends, spacing yourselves evenly across its width. Drop your biscuits in the stream at the same time.

By watching the way the biscuits move you can find out which part of the stream flows fastest.

Streamers

Water in a stream moves in very mysterious ways. If you want to see how it moves, one easy way is to make the streamers shown in the picture on the left.

Use different coloured ribbons and tie them to a cane, each the same distance apart. When you dip the cane in the water, the streamers will trail out with the current and show you just how the water is moving.

Choose a shallow stream or one with a firm bank and see what the streamers show near the outside and near the inside of bends.

Natural streamers

In large rivers, it is not safe to wade and you will have to study the water from the banks or from bridges. However, you can make use of natural streamers, such as water plants, to show you what is happening to the flow.

The water plants trail out in an even pattern showing you that the water is flowing quickly and evenly across the channel.

The plants are swept towards the outside of the bend, showing that this is where the water flows fastest and where the bank is likely to be most quickly worn away.

What rivers carry

Landshapes are made when a river cuts into (or erodes) the land, or when it drops (or **deposits**) material that it has been carrying.

The main materials of a river bed are mud, silt, sand, gravel and pebbles. Large boulders and rocks are only moved during times of great flood.

These are ripples on a sandy stream bed.

Bottle sampler

Streams and rivers flow fast enough to prevent the smallest particles from settling out on the bottom. You can sample this material using a jar dipped into the water.

A fairly wide-necked jar will let water and particles flow in evenly. Angle the jar slightly upwards so the air escapes as the water enters.

If you want to see how much mud was in the water you can pour the contents through a coffee filter placed in a kitchen funnel, then let the paper dry out. You can keep dried filters with dates on to see how the muddiness of the river samples changes from one day to another.

Mud and silt

These are the finest rock grains of all. They will only settle to the bottom in still water such as in lakes. Here you see mud and silt still muddying the water in this collecting jar.

Bed trap

If you want to see how much sand, gravel and pebbles are moved across a stream bed, put a seed tray in the bed of a stream and weight it down with two bricks. Leave it for a few days then return to see how much material has been washed into it.

Sand
This is the finest rock material that normally makes a river bed. It is moved along by the river in a kind of hopping motion and very often makes ripples on the river bed.

Gravel
This is larger in size than sand and is sometimes found where the river is flowing strongly.

Pebbly bed
In many stream and river beds pebbles are found on the surface. They can only be carried when the river is flowing very fast, such as during a flood. At this time the water rolls them along the bed.

Pebbly beds are often exposed at times of low water, when they are called shoals.

Rivers of many stages

Rivers change in character quite dramatically between their **sources** in the hills or mountains and their **mouths** at the sea or in a lake. For example, the main river tumbles over boulders on a rocky bed near its source, but as you follow it out of the hills and into the plains, the river begins to swing from side to side or break up into many islands. Finally, as it nears its mouth, the river wanders almost aimlessly in a broad gentle valley.

This is a youthful river with a rocky bed and many large boulders in the channel.

Youthful rivers

It takes time for rivers to make their mark on the landscape. To begin with all they seem able to do is to cut deeply into the rock.

Rivers with rocky beds are easy to spot because they have foaming, gurgling water – called white water – along their paths.

This is a mature river with a wide cultivated flood plain.

Mature rivers

These make winding, or meandering, paths across a belt of flat land called a flood plain. The flood plain is the area that becomes flooded when, after a period of heavy rain or snowmelt, the river bursts its banks. You can see the floodplain clearly in this picture – farmers have used it for pasture and cultivation.

During a flood, much fine material is carried onto the flood plain where it settles out, adding a thin layer to the soil of the flood plain. This process is repeated many thousands of times during the life of a river and gradually thick deposits build up that completely cover the rocky floor of the valley. Mature rivers rarely flow on a rock bed.

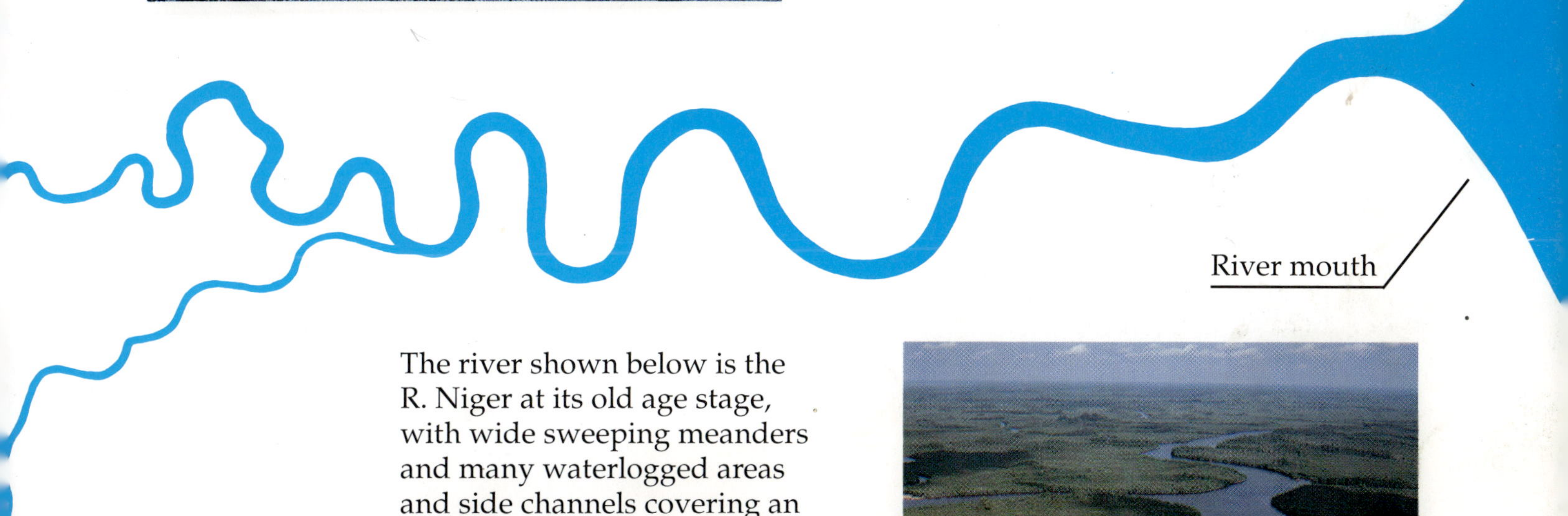

The river shown below is the R. Niger at its old age stage, with wide sweeping meanders and many waterlogged areas and side channels covering an almost flat coastal lowland.

Old age rivers

As a river reaches its mouth, the course becomes almost flat. In their old age stage, rivers move over thick spreads of fine sand or silt.

Old age rivers are often tidal and the channels are at their widest. The world's biggest river, the Amazon in South America, is over 160 kilometres across and it is tidal for over 1000 kilometres from the sea!

Chapter 2

Rivers in hills and mountains

Where water tumbles

In its young stage a river will carve the most spectacular landshapes.

When streams and rivers flow very quickly, such as when they are in mountainous country, no material can settle on the bed. A rocky bed is not protected from the bumping and bouncing of the pebbles that are whisked over it by the speedy water and it is soon scoured into interesting shapes.

River's sandpaper

Pebbles that make potholes are round and smooth because they have had all the rough edges worn away as they drilled into the river bed.

You can see how quickly this happens by using some sugar cubes. Put several sugar cubes into a jar and close the lid. Shake them about for a few seconds and then look at the sugar. There will be a lot of loose sugar grains. These are like the sands of grains carried by a river; there will also be smaller and more rounded 'cubes'; these are like the pebbles bounced along a river bed.

Potholes

In some places the water swirls round and round, and if pebbles get caught in this swirling motion they begin to wear the bed away, drilling a deep pot-shaped hole.

Potholes can be several metres deep. In some rivers, especially those that move down very steep courses, one pothole follows another to give spectacular landshapes like the one shown on the opposite page. In other places the potholes are much smaller and they spread out over the river bed, giving it a 'pepper-pot' appearance.

In many potholes you can see stones trapped inside. They will not escape until they have worn themselves down to sand, and by this time they will have deepened the pothole further.

1. Small potholes form in the river bed. They are easy to see in dry weather when the water level is low.

Tumbler test

If you can borrow a stone-polishing machine you can see how real stones are worn smooth. Because of their toughness, stone polishing takes weeks to achieve a good finish. See what happens to the stones each day and take out a few each time. Now make a display of each group of stones to show how rounding happens with time.

2. Sometimes potholes grow to become as wide as the entire stream.

3. On rare occasions potholes cut a gorge. Notice how the sides of this gorge have a smooth, rounded look – they are the sides of old potholes.

SCALE

Waterfalls and rapids

Waterfalls and rapids form wherever tough bands of rock lie across the river's path.

The most spectacular waterfalls occur where there are large rivers and thick level sheets of rock. Rapids are found where the bands of rock lie at an angle to the river, causing the water to be broken, but never to fall from one level to another.

This gorge has been cut by the waterfall. A gorge may be many kilometers long, marking where the waterfall used to be.

You can almost count the number of tough rock bands that make the rapids at the bottom of this deep valley.

How a waterfall changes the land

The place where water falls over a hard rock band is called a lip. As the water crashes to the valley below, a mixture of water and stones scours a deep pool, called the plunge pool.

As the plunge pool grows it cuts under the waterfall's lip, causing blocks to fall from the lip. In this way the waterfall cuts its way further upstream.

In the front of the picture to the right you can see the wide gorge that has been cut by many centuries of water scouring. Frost and other agents of the weather widen the gorge long after the waterfall has retreated.

Waterfall lip
Plunge pool, where the full force of the falling water can smash rocks and undercut the lip.

Rivers that shape islands

Some rivers have pebbly banks and beds. These rivers are wide and shallow and they often have many pebbly islands in their channels.

Rivers with pebbly islands are called **braided** rivers because the water in the channel has to cross back and forth, just like the strands of braided hair.

Sand and pebbles do not stick together like clay and silt. This is why sand and pebbles do not make high banks, but collapse to a gentle angle. Braided channels are usually very wide.

Braided rivers have many sandy or pebbly islands that split the water into many streams. The islands show most clearly when the river has little water in it.

This braided river is in a mountainous area. You can see clearly the way the water splits around islands and then comes together again.

River of sand

You can find out how wide, shallow rivers work by making a sand tank model. Make sure you have some way of collecting the water that runs out of the end of the model.

The model needs to be as long as possible. Ask a grown-up to make a shallow tray of wood and line it with plastic sheet.

Fill the tray with clean sand to a little below the top, then get a hose and run water into the top of the tank. Soon a river will form.

Look carefully at how the water erodes the outer banks and deposits material on the inside of the bends. You should also be able to see sand grains hopping along the bed.

Experiment with different amounts of water and different slopes of the tank.

Chapter 3
Rivers on plains

Rivers of twists and turns

Most of the world's lowland rivers twist and turn as they make their way to the sea. Each river curve is called a meander.

Meanders are made by the water as it flows down a slope. How much a river twists always matches the landscape it flows through: large rivers, like the Mississippi, have meanders that are many kilometres across, but even small streams that flow on a desk top can twist!

A meander
A meander is a sweeping river curve. When the curve changes direction it is the start of a new meander. You can therefore count several meanders in this picture.

Rivers cut the curves

The curves in a river are always under attack by the water. The water flows quickly round the outside curve of the meander and here it eats into the bank, carrying material away. But at the same time there is slack water on the inside of the curve and any material carried to this region is dropped.

Because cutting on one bank happens at the same time as filling-in on the opposite bank, a river never changes its width even though it changes its course.

The outside edge of a curve is called a **river cliff** because it is often very steep.

The inside curve builds up material. This is called a **bar**.

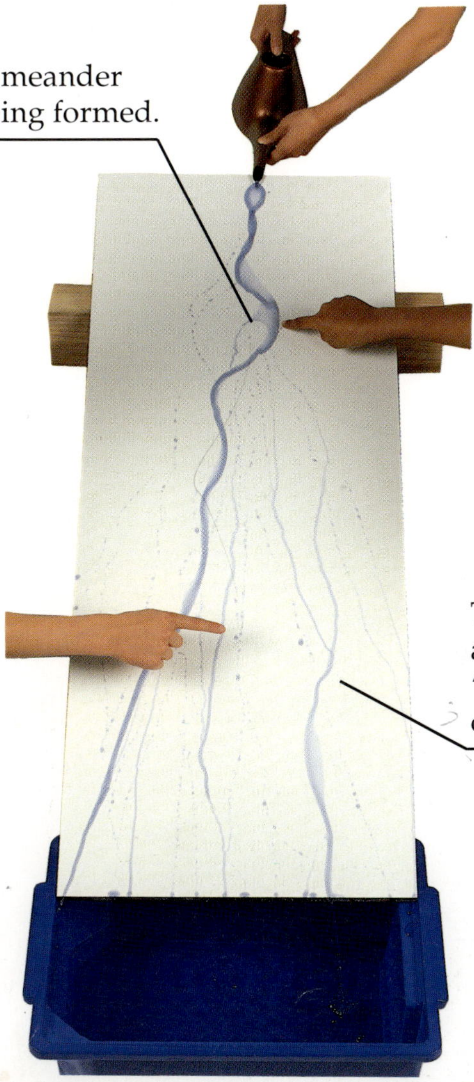

A meander being formed.

The trail of a previous 'river' for comparison.

Make meanders

You can see meanders form and change shape easily. All you need is a clean dry flat desk or kitchen table. Make sure it has a water-resistant surface.

Prop one end of the table on some thick books so that you have a long slope. This will be the course of the river. You will also need a large tray under the lower end of the table to catch water.

Use a jug with a pouring spout and carefully pour water that has been coloured with blue food dye onto the top part of the table. Pour just enough to get a continuous flow. The water will run down, and as it does so it will begin to meander.

Try to pour evenly for several minutes and you will find that the 'river' shifts its track, gradually snaking down the table surface.

Cutting new courses

During flooding rivers find it much easier to flow in new directions. In general the rule is, the more water there is in a channel, the less the water twists and turns. This means that a flooding river may cut a new, less twisting channel across the twists and turns of the normal channel. Then, when the river level rises again it may well follow the new course instead of going back to its former position.

The course of the river today.

Oxbows

As rivers cut into the soft materials of the floodplain, they gradually shift course. In general, the steeper the river's course, the bigger the meanders become. At their most extreme they make huge loops, or goosenecks, which almost touch. Goosenecks are frequently cut off when rivers are in flood.

The abandoned goosenecks are called oxbows, and they may remain filled with water for a long while after they have been abandoned. But as one gooseneck is cut off, so another begins to form in a never-ending sequence as shown by the changes of the river in these pictures.

Some goosenecks are cut through, others begin to develop.

The course of the river hundreds of years ago.

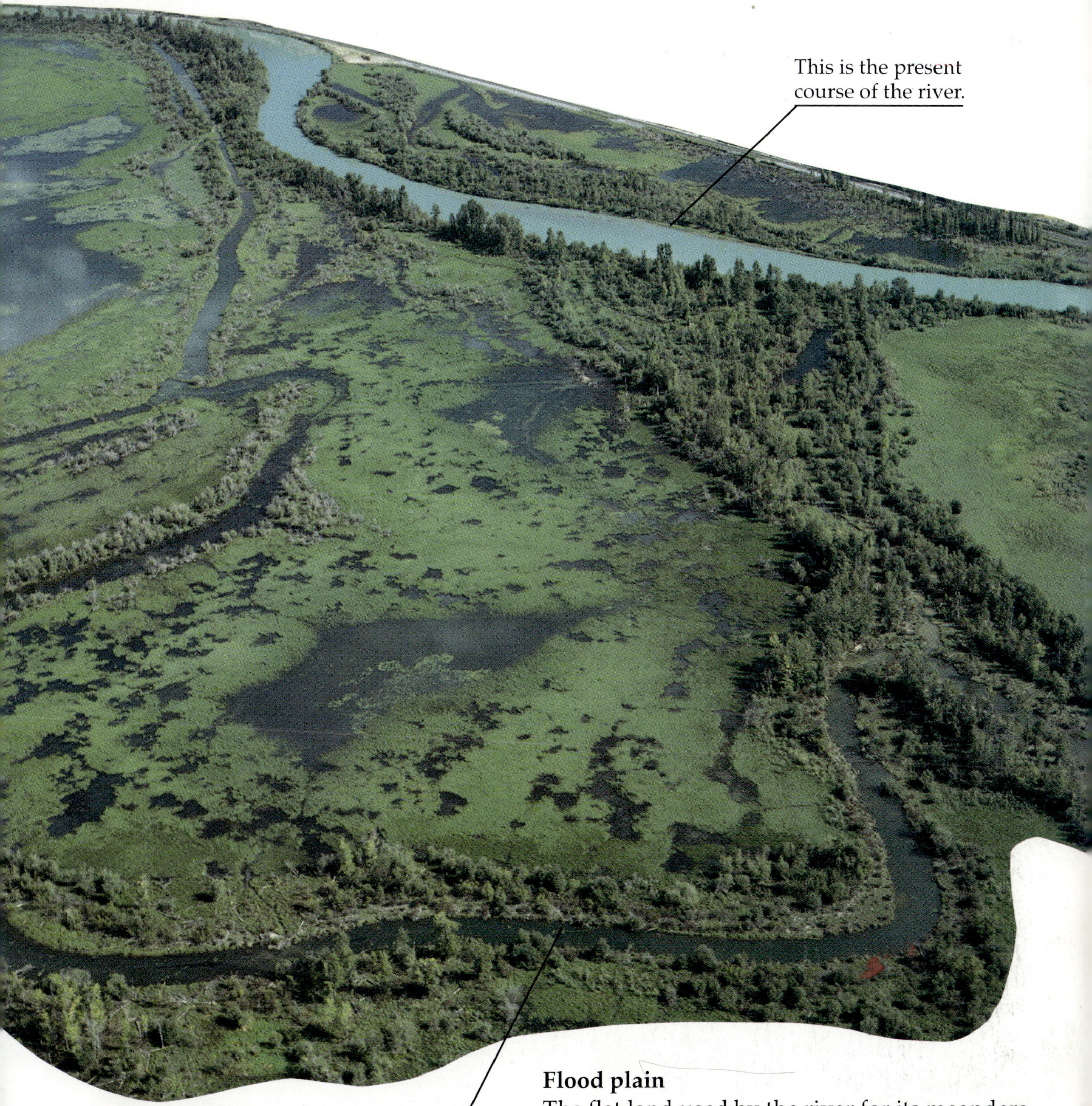

Flood plain

The flat land used by the river for its meanders or braids is always likely to flood when there is a lot of rain or when snow melts quickly.

In this picture you can see how the flood plain is naturally flat and marshy. Flood plains near your home may not, however, be marshy as they are often drained and used by farmers because the soil is extremely fertile.

What floods do

When rivers are in flood they can make big changes to the shape of the land. Sometimes they drop sheets of clay and silt (mud) over the bottom of the valley. Flat flood plains in valley bottoms have been shaped this way by thousands of past floods.

Sand and pebbles are often dropped near to the channel and they build natural walls, or **levees**.

Rivers often change their courses during floods and at this time people with houses on flood plains discover that rivers can change landshapes very quickly!

The main material dropped by a flooding river is thick mud. You can see mud coating the pebbles in this picture of a dry river bed. If it builds up to be thick enough, this mud will form fertile soils and may be used as farmland.

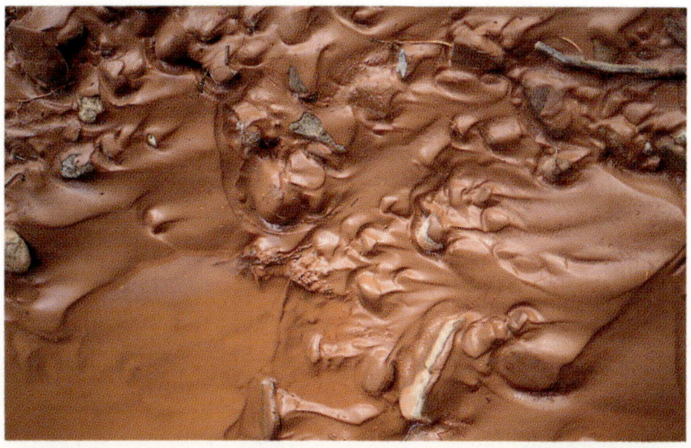

The picture above was taken looking straight down on some houses on a flood plain. It shows how the river changed its course during a storm and chose a route through the houses. You can see the channels clearly.

Just imagine how difficult it must have been to clear up the debris left behind by the flood!

The power of a river to change the shape of the land shows clearly when rivers flood near to homes. How many recent changes to the flood plain can you spot in the picture above?

The story in the river banks

A river bank is like the pages of a history book. It keeps a record of many of the events that have happened over hundreds of years. By looking at the bank you can tell just what a river has been doing.

When the river is in flood it spills over its banks and drops fine material over the flood plain. This top layer of clay may have been made this way.

This layer of pebbles was dropped by the river on the outside of a bend where the current is strong.

Building banks

Many river banks show layers, some fine and others coarse and pebbly. Pebbly materials are the only ones that can stand up to fast currents, fine materials get dropped in places of slack water.

As the river swings back and forth, each part of the floodplain gets a share of fast and slack water. How often it happens is shown by the story in the river banks.

This part of the bed has a great assortment of stones and fine particles. Perhaps they were dropped in the channel after a flood.

This is the level of the river when it is in flood and spilling over its banks.

Your local history
Visit a stream with a grown-up and some friends. See if you can spot layers of coarse and fine material. If you look in the stream you may also be able to see fast and slack regions.

This is the level of the river for much of the year.

This fine mud was dropped by a river on the inside of a bend where the current is slack.

Chapter 4

Rivers of the world

The Nile

This is the world's longest river, flowing for over 6670 kilometres through the countries of north east Africa. Most people think of the Nile as an 'Egyptian' river, but it begins far to the south, near the Equator.

The Nile has two main sources, one, which starts in Lake Victoria and is known as the White Nile, the other, which starts in the Ethiopian Highlands is called the Blue Nile.

The White and Blue Niles join at the Sudanese capital of Khartoum. From here the Nile flows through desert and no more water enters.

During its next 1800 kilometres the river sweeps in a great S-shaped path. On it lie some famous rapids (or cataracts). The most famous is at the city of Aswan, shown in the picture below, now the site of a high dam and a reservoir called Lake Nasser which has flooded part of the Nile valley.

Below Cairo the river has dropped vast amounts of mud and it splits up into many channels, called distributaries, to feed this huge **delta**.

Cairo is at the head of the Nile Delta.

Between the Aswan cataract and Egypt's capital city of Cairo, the river keeps a single broad channel through the desert.

The source of the Blue Nile is Lake Tana in Ethiopia. The picture below shows the huge waterfall at the outlet of the lake at Bahir Dhar.

Aswan

Lake Nasser

The Amazon

This is the world's biggest river even though, at 6450 kilometres, it is not quite as long as Africa's Nile. This is because the Amazon is fed by a network of smaller, or **tributary**, rivers that cover more than half of South America – over one twentieth of the world's entire land area!

When it reaches the Atlantic Ocean, the Amazon is carrying more than one fifth of all the water that flows in the world's rivers.

There are many sources to the Amazon. Most lie in the west of the continent, on the flanks of the giant Andes mountain range in areas that are tropical forest. In these places rain falls throughout the year and it soaks readily into the soils to feed the river. This is the only place where waterfalls occur in the Amazon basin.

Except in the Andes mountains, the Amazon flows in a giant low lying basin, the vast majority of it being less than 150 metres above sea level. This means that there are rarely valley sides to be seen, and the river simply winds aimlessly over a huge floodplain. This picture shows Minaus, about 1200 km from the mouth.

Near the sea the river is over 160 kilometres wide and its mouth is studded with low muddy islands. When you stand on one bank it is therefore impossible to see the other side.

The tides, and salty water, reach upstream for 1000 kilometres, which is farther than any other river in the world.

New words

bar
a deposit of pebbles or sand that builds up in slack water on the inside bank of a curve in a river channel

braid
a temporary island that splits up the water in a river channel. Braids occur in large numbers and are changed in size and shape by each flood. By contrast, islands occur in small numbers and do not change after floods

channel
the shallow trench that has been cut by a river or stream

delta
the fan-shaped deposits that build up where a river enters a lake or sea

deposits
any material that has been carried by a river and which is then dropped. Clay, silt, sand and pebbles are all materials dropped, or deposited, by a river at times of slack water

erode
the wearing away of the land. Rivers mainly erode their beds by using the sandpaper-like action caused as pebbles and sand bounce along the bed. The force of the water alone is enough to erode the bank of a river

levee
a natural bank that builds up beside some very silty rivers during floods. As the rivers spill from their channels much of the material they are carrying is dropped and this gradually builds into a bank. The Mississippi is famous for its levees which are several metres high

meander
the natural curves that are made by a lowland river as it flows along

mouth
the place where the river reaches the sea. Sometimes the river mouth is deep and wide, this is called an estuary. Other rivers build up deltas at their mouths

pothole
the deeply scoured pits that are made as pebbles are swirled round and round on a river bed

oxbow
the abandoned curve of a river. An oxbow often contains ponded water and this is called an oxbow lake

rapids
stretches where the river rushes and tumbles over exposed rocks

river cliff
the steep bank on the outside curve of a meander. It is made steep by the scouring action of the water

source
the place where the river first begins to flow. Some rivers begin as flowing springs. More commonly rivers start with water seeping through soils to form a muddy patch

tributary
a smaller river that flows into a main river

waterfall
a place where a river spills over a level band of rock and drops through the air. The smallest waterfalls are no more than steps a metre or so high, the largest are nearly 1000 metres high

Index